Jobs If You Like...

Computers

Charlotte Guillain

www.raintreepublishers.co.uk
Visit our website to find out more information about Raintree books.

To order:

☎ Phone 0845 6044371

🖹 Fax +44 (0) 1865 312263

🖳 Email myorders@raintreepublishers.co.uk

Customers from outside the UK please telephone +44 1865 312262

Raintree is an imprint of Capstone Global Library Limited, a company incorporated in England and Wales having its registered office at 7 Pilgrim Street, London, EC4V 6LB – Registered company number: 6695582

Edited by Rebecca Rissman, Daniel Nunn, and Adrian Vigliano
Designed by Steve Mead
Picture research by Mica Brancic
Originated by Capstone Global Library
Printed and bound in China by South China Printing Company

ISBN 978 1 406 24065 8 (hardback)
16 15 14 13 12
10 9 8 7 6 5 4 3 2 1

British Library Cataloguing in Publication Data
Guillain, Charlotte.
Jobs for kids who like computers.
004'.023-dc22
A full catalogue record for this book is available from the British Library.

Acknowledgements
We would like to thank the following for permission to reproduce photographs: [select]

Cover photograph of [select] reproduced with permission of [select].

We would like to thank [name of organization or individual] for [pronoun] invaluable help in the preparation of this book.

Every effort has been made to contact copyright holders of material reproduced in this book. Any omissions will be rectified in subsequent printings if notice is given to the publisher.

Contents

Some words are shown in bold, **like this**. You can find out what they mean by looking in the glossary.

Why do computers matter?

How often do you use computers? You probably use them all the time! Today there are computers in cars, telephones, televisions, and many other things.

People use the computer inside their mobile phone for many things.

Many people use computers to work, find information, and have fun. There are lots of exciting jobs that use computers. Read this book to find out about some of these amazing jobs. Maybe there is a job here that you would love to do?

Computer games can be lots of fun.

Be a website designer

You see websites whenever you use the Internet. You can play games, get information, or buy things on websites. A website designer thinks about what the people using a website will need.

People use websites for many things every day.

If you were a website designer, you would plan all the **web pages** on a website. You would think about the words and pictures the website needs. Then you would put the website together on a computer and make sure it works properly.

Websites need to be quick and easy for people to use.

Be a games developer

Imagine playing computer games all day! If you were a games developer, you would think of new ideas for computer games. Games developers need to enjoy playing games themselves.

People will always be looking for new computer games to play.

Some games developers write a **computer program** to make a new game work. Others design the way the game looks and feels. Then people need to test the game to make sure it works properly before people play it.

Games developers need to use different computer programs.

Be an IT support technician

We all need help when things go wrong! If you were an IT support technician, you would help other people who use computers. You would have to find problems and fix them.

IT support technicians have to explain to people how **computer programs** work.

IT support technicians sometimes work in teams to help solve computer problems.

IT support technicians need to understand the way different computers work. They need to know how to solve many problems. They are also good at explaining things and training other people.

Be a computer graphics animator

Imagine bringing cartoon characters to life! If you were a computer graphics animator, you would use a computer to make **animations**. Computer graphics can show incredible things that couldn't happen in real life in cartoons, films, and games.

Computer graphics animators get their ideas from stories and their own imaginations.

A computer graphics animator designs **3D** images on a computer. Then the **computer program** makes the images move and change. Some computer graphics look like real animals and people.

Some computer graphics animators use physical models and computer programs together.

Be an electrical engineer

Do you like gadgets? If you were an electrical **engineer**, you would design and make electronic **equipment** such as mobile phones, televisions, and computers. You would need to make sure things work properly and are easy to use.

Electrical engineers fix any problems with new equipment.

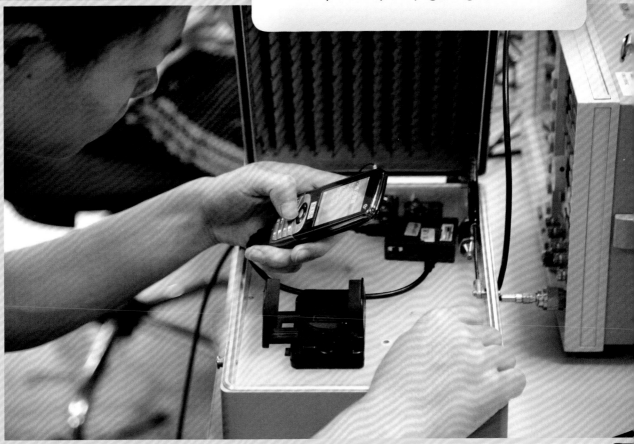

Electrical engineers make many everyday gadgets work.

Electrical engineers can use computers to design new equipment. When they have built the equipment they need to test it and solve any problems. They need to understand how computers work.

Be a robotics designer

Would you like to create your own robot? If you were a robotics designer, you would have ideas for new robots. You would think of new ways robots can help us.

Robotics designers make robots work in the best way.

Some robots help the army to clear away bombs. Other robots build machinery, explore other planets, or help doctors do operations. Robotics designers need to use computers to make robots work.

These robots are building new cars.

Be a forensic scientist

If you were a forensic scientist, you would help the police to solve crimes. You would look at **evidence** to work out who criminals are. You would use computers in many different ways.

Forensic scientists have to look for evidence first.

Forensic scientists help examine evidence after it has been collected.

Forensic scientists can use computer **databases** to identify fingerprints, blood, and other things. They can use **computer modelling** to help them solve problems. Sometimes they find evidence on criminals' mobile phones or computers.

Be an automotive engineer

Would you like to design and make cars? If you were an automotive **engineer**, you might work out how computers can be used in cars. Many cars use computers to open windows, tell the driver where to go, and keep the driver cool or warm.

Most new cars use computers in many different ways.

Automotive engineers come up with new ideas for using computers in cars. They have to test these ideas to make sure they work properly. They have to work out how to fix any problems.

Engineers find new ways to make cars better.

Be a meteorologist

Do you want to see into the future? If you were a meteorologist, you would forecast the weather and study Earth's **climate**. You would collect information about the weather from all over the world.

Meteorologists put information into computers to find out what the weather is going to do.

Computers help to find patterns in the weather.

Meteorologists use **computer modelling** to see what the weather is probably going to be like. Sometimes they make new **computer programs** to forecast the weather. This can help farmers, pilots, and many other people.

23

Be an oceanographer

If you were an oceanographer, you would explore the world under the oceans. Some oceanographers study sea animals and plants. Others look at **pollution** in the oceans or study the bottom of the ocean.

Oceanographers can spend a lot of time under water!

Oceanographers use computers
to make sense of their data.

Oceanographers put the information they
gather on computers. They also use computers
to understand and present **data**. Some
oceanographers use computer models to show
what the ocean floor looks like.

Choosing the right job for you

When you decide what you want to do when you grow up, don't just think about school subjects. Think about what you enjoy doing. If you enjoy playing computer games then you might like a job designing or testing games.

If you have a good imagination and can solve problems then maybe you could be a robotics designer. There are so many interesting jobs using computers that there is something to suit everyone.

Five things you couldn't do without computers
- Use a mobile phone
- Use a remote control
- Microwave a snack
- Play a video game
- Listen to an MP3 player

Computer job chart

If you want to find out more about any of the jobs in this book, start here:

	Automotive engineer	Computer graphics animator	Electrical engineer	Forensic scientist	
You need to:	Like cars	Be creative	Understand how things work	Look carefully at details	
Best thing about it:	Making cars work in new ways!	Bringing characters to life!	Making cool new gadgets!	Solving crimes!	

	Games developer	IT support technician	Meteorologist	Oceanographer	Robotics designer	Website designer
	Enjoy games	Be good at listening	Be interested in weather and climate	Be interested in the oceans	Come up with new ideas	Think about what people need
	You get to play at work!	Helping people!	Predicting the future!	You go to the beach a lot!	Designing your own robot!	Making something people find useful!

Glossary

3D three-dimensional, looking very life-like

animation cartoon made up of moving images

climate usual weather in a place

computer modelling when a computer works out what is likely to happen in a situation

computer program instructions given to a computer to make it do a job

data facts, figures, and other information

database collection of information on a computer

engineer person who uses science and maths to make tools, buildings, and machines

equipment something made to be used in a special way

evidence proof that something happened or how it happened

pollution waste that is harmful to the environment

web page content on a screen that is part of a website

Find out more

The Science Museum
www.sciencemuseum.org.uk/onlinestuff/subjects/
communications_and_computing.aspx
Visit the website of the Science Museum in London
to find out more about what computers can do.

Pixar Animation Studios
www.pixar.com/howwedoit/index.html
Watch how Pixar make animated films such as
Toy Story 3 using computer generated images.

Young Engineers
www.youngeng.org/home.asp
Find out more about all types of engineering.

Index